Thank you for your brilliance, dear poe[...] [...] us an oracle born from
a digital wave in all its entanglements,
This living poem enfolds shards of its
the poet's insistence on how we under
recent falls.

Cat Chong is a thrilling new voice in
a poetic that is experimental and ali
read.

— Joelle Taylor

A necessary hymnal for and from the collective moment 'when we could no longer
tell what was cake and what / wasn't', Cat Chong's *712 Stanza Homes for the Sun*
sings with and in praise of density, immediacy, specificity and with a canniness of
the uncanniness of digital intimacies and (dis)integrations. With room for Zooms,
notes, photographs, cats, climate chaos tweets and other materialities, this collection
is a home for ephemera in its full sense of what makes up our days, dailiness, daylight,
containing multitudes as the cotyledon stores sunlight. These poems are — and
instruct us to — 'seed messages', nourishing (to use Lola Olufemi's term) packets
that contain many future poetries within them through the honour they offer to
substance/s, traces, patterns, crumbs of what could be. Recognising that 'we don't own
/ the vector along which data moves', including within our own material existences,
Chong models poetry as the weight of a refusing body on the levers of production
and social reproduction, a cripqueer disruptor that moves, through a riot of language,
against borders and controls. As they say, multilayering with irony and desire:

    —it was all still a version of happiness—the lexicon of

    the age—it announced us as small fragments—of larger crises—

— So Mayer

712 Stanza Homes For The Sun is a vibrant and innovative record of the pandemic
unlike any other — found text and images, tweets, emails, photographs, quotations
from writers and loved ones interweave with fragmented narration and the
intervention of roving macaques — so that not just gender and genre and sickness are
queered, as Chong writes, but the pandemic itself. These poems are equally playful
and eviscerating — drawing together disability justice, climate justice, critiques of
colonialism, capitalism, state control and genocide — yet still finding shimmering
beauty in this world in crisis. Chong's is a unique and vital voice in poetry — 'bearing
witness to the ways in which we all fall apart'.

— Polly Atkin

These are startlingly original mappings, sensings, soundings, of what it means to live in
these desperate times. The poetics here may be disruptive, dissociative, discontinuous,
but these poems are also making subterranean connections between what seem
disparate and fragmented, discovering narratives between places, times and lives. These
are border-crossing, genre-bending prose poems, boldly transgressive, their liminal and
cosmopolitan lens producing a new cartography of the realities and border-zones we
now inhabit.

— Boey Kim Cheng

Also by Cat Chong

Plain Air   (Broken Sleep Books, 2021)

712 STANZA HOMES FOR THE SUN

Cat Chong is a a poet, publisher, and PhD student at Nanyang Technological University, Singapore where their research considers the intersections between gender, genre, disability, and chronic illness. Their debut pamphlet *Plain Air: An Apology in Transit* was published by Broken Sleep Books in 2021.

ISBN: 978-1-915760-04-3

The author has asserted their right to be identified as the author of this Work in accordance with the Copyright, Designs and Patents Act 1988

Cover designed by Aaron Kent

Edited & Typeset by Aaron Kent

Broken Sleep Books Ltd
Rhydwen
Talgarreg
Ceredigion
SA44 4HB

Broken Sleep Books Ltd
Fair View
St Georges Road
Cornwall
PL26 7YH

Contents

712 Stanza Homes for the Sun

Cat Chong

I am eager to re-read and re-write my life as an ongoing poem, but no longer in linear time.

— Mary Jean Chan, *Queerness As Translation: From Linear Time To Playtime*

Imagine that all you have done to form your practice as a poet has extended itself outward toward the heavens.

— Anne Boyer, *A Handbook of Disappointed Fate*

There are ways of acknowledging influence and models, by ingestion, by assimilation, by one's total absorption in the material.

— Caroline Bergvall, *VIA*

That is, to assemble large-scale constructions out of the smallest and most precisely cut components.

— Walter Benjamin, *The Arcades Project*

i guess i'm falling apart, i'll just / sew myself back together but will it last? / please take a piece of me back home, each piece / is anti-war and don't pay your rent, in fact / remember: property is robbery, give everybody / everything, other birds walk this way too

— Bernadette Mayer, *Walking Like a Robin*

Once the young poet [Wallace Stevens], contemplating suicide, went to the water's edge, but he was so distracted by the tidal debris that he put aside his depressing thoughts and began to write about garbage instead.

— Andrew S. Gross, *Wallace Stevens: Anecdote and Lyric*

[A poem] is fucking proof that somebody was not afraid for a little while.

— Franz Wright, *Two Years With Franz*

"An essay that becomes a lyric, […] is an essay that has killed itself." A prose line can stave off this death for as long as the seams of its syntax hold. And when they fail to hold, a run-on can seem less a sloppy piece of grammar than a desperate act to stay alive.

— John D'Agata, *The Next American Essay*

24 ———— Craft teaches us that style is never finished. The present, borrowed or perhaps inherited as our material project, is never finished. There is always something to do.

25 ————

26 ———— CRAFT, AGAINST DEATH.

—in so much pain—the bombs would weep pumpkin pip seed messages denoting time the pip boi counting units—of radiation the radar a nautical investigation—the commons are here at the beginnings of water—"I'll be right back I'm just going to get a black pen"—the root word for blacken is the same word for bleach bleak and total whiteness—to some of our most sacred texts genre doesn't really apply—when I write says—Mary Reufle in *Madness, Rack, and Honey*—my gender becomes genre[1]—to some of our most sacred texts gender doesn't really apply—swerves off the radar—out of algorhythmic fidelity—to be untraceably genred untrackably gendered—is to live untargetably as in things—as the mirrors are blackened and bleached—so absorption voids the image—this is still an archive and looking for a place to hide—perhaps I should not be writing at all a poetics of pips that knows how long I have left—to plant or search for soil—a kinship to acknowledge the land—and the possibility for grounding—whether it'll emerge or look back in laughter or cold water—I have no interest in weapons or their complicity—I am love hungry—I want to reply to you once I understand where the light is coming from—blur with me—I have failed the song of living—blue with me—I finished that poem and the next day my brother died—said Peter Gizzi on day 395 the 29th of January 2021—on the 1st of February Lisa Robertson's Instagram answers back[2]—in an image of *26 Theses On Craft* she writes—24 there is always something to do—25 blank—26 CRAFT, AGAINST DEATH—

1.   (Ruefle, 2012, p. 289)
2.   (Robertson, 2021)

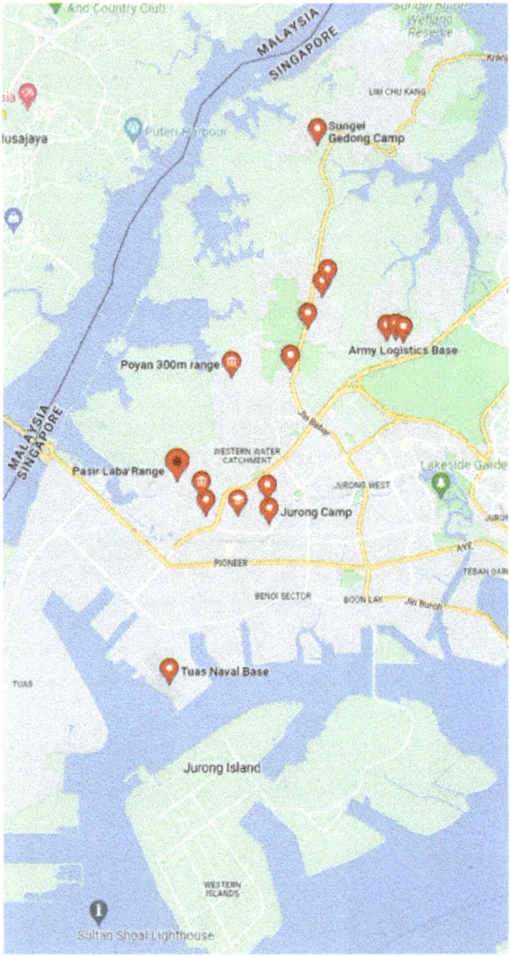

And Country Club
MALAYSIA
SINGAPORE
LIM CHU KANG
Sungei Gedong Camp
Puteri Harbour
Army Logistics Base
Poyan 300m range
MALAYSIA
SINGAPORE
WESTERN WATER CATCHMENT
Pasir Laba Range
Jurong Camp
JURONG WEST
Lakeside Garden
PIONEER
BENOI SECTOR
BOON LAY
Jln Buroh
Tuas Naval Base
TUAS
Jurong Island
WESTERN ISLANDS
Sultan Shoal Lighthouse

400.   —I've been keeping count of the days—

—since the 1ˢᵗ of January 2020—counting the multiple precarities
of "the vulnerable"—waiting to be allowed to see my family—my
partner—my friends—the list gets longer each time—I can still
hear the bombs—the military jets—the live firing from the Ponyan
gun range that's under a mile away—the Pasir Laba range that's
a mile and a half away—and because I cannot tell the sound from
which—and because an NS National Service training institute
marks a perimeter just beyond the storm drain along the north
western perimeter of campus—and an SAF—Singapore Air Force
base—borders the south—and because the military holds all the
land west[3]—on every blank map—perhaps regardless—whether it's
the record or the countdown the dread is still the same—perhaps
this is still anecdotal—an unsubstantiated structure of belief with
which to convey the unverifiable—the legal—institutional—
empirical—subterfuge—Jurong Island is just over 4 miles
south—Shell—Chevron—BP—ExxonMobil—the Petrochemical
Corporation of Singapore—and many more occupy the reclaimed
artificial land[4]—taxi drivers tell me it's used for toxic chemical
manufacturing—but that's just the rumour—the eavesdrop—the
goss—the tone is still the same—Jurong Island—chronic pain—
military property—invisible disability—believe me—please—the
scent of burnt cocoa—the Cadbury's chocolate factory—ADM
cocoa—Khong Guan Biscuit Factory—the poultry farms in Sungei
Tengah—all hang in the air at night—

---

3.   (Google, 2021)
4.   (Wikipedia, 2021)

Jurong Island

From Wikipedia, the free encyclopedia

Jurong Island is an island located to the southwest of the main island of Singapore. It was formed from the amalgamation of seven offshore islands, the islands of Pulau Ayer Chawan, Pulau Ayer Merbau, Pulau Merlimau, Pulau Pesek, Pulau Pesek Kechil (also called Terumbu Pesek), Pulau Sakra (which was a previous merger of Pulau Sakra and Pulau Bakau), Pulau Seraya, Pulau Meskol, Pulau Mesemut Laut, Pulau Mesemut Darat and Anak Pulau. This was done through Singapore's land reclamation efforts. Land reclamation on Jurong Island was completed on 25 September 2009, 20 years earlier than scheduled. Pulau Buaya was joined to Jurong Island via reclamation in 2010. Jurong Island forms a land area of about 32 km^2 (12 sq mi) from an initial area of less than 10 km^2 (4 sq mi), and is the largest of Singapore's outlying islands.

Jurong Island

Jurong Island, photographed in February 2011

Location of Jurong Island within Singapore

Geography	
Location	Southeast Asia
Coordinates	1°16'0"N 103°41'45"E
Archipelago	Malay Archipelago
Area	32 km^2 (12 sq mi)
Administration	
	Singapore
Region	West Region
Planning Area	Western Islands
CDC	• South West CDC
Town council	• West Coast Town Council
Constituency	• West Coast GRC
Member of Parliament	• Foo Mee Har

Contents [hide]

History [edit]

The outlying islands of Pulau Ayer Chawan, Pulau Ayer Merbau, Pulau Merlimau and Pulau Seraya were used to house fishing communities comprising small villages up to the 1960s. The villagers lived in Malay-style wooden stilt houses on the palm-fringed islands. Between the late-1960s and early-1970s, three big oil companies planned to house their facilities on Pulau Ayer Chawan for Esso, Pulau Merlimau for Singapore Refinery Company and Pulau Pesek for Mobil Oil.

The Government of Singapore then took the opportunity to grow the petrochemical industry as a choice that would significantly produce economic growth. This was proven by the success of starting off the petroleum industries in the 1970s.

—the way we organise energy in space aligns us in dialogue with
our being with the world—I'm misquoting Pessoa—it's all the same
line—all you have to do is—put quotations around it sensemaking—
movement in a state of being intrinsic to water—perhaps we'll
never pass through the same—never stand in the same pain
twice—I cannot write out the singular desire to escape the body—
one of the earliest pioneers of cyberspace was a lyricist for The
Grateful Dead—I want out of my body as bad as that old white
man in the earliest stages of the internet[5]—a liquid self-effacing
onto the street—I don't want to be—medical sloganeering—an
industrial habitat—or the clarifying mechanism of the moon—fuck
me or gut me it's all the same address—if one grows sentimental
when in pain I must live like a nostalgia—millimetres away from
my skin—I am fleshed out of painkillers in the kingdom of this
world—part of doing this is not wanting to do this—I don't know if
language will be warmer—living one degree north of the equator—
where pain never comes in with the cold—where there's no such
thing as winter—and the monsoons too have a spell—I don't want
to make this thesis a violent spectacle of my undiagnosed survival—
the truth makes me visible—to enquire—after pain's manifold
geometries—exceeding all predictions—pain knows me before I
do—I am—trying to cultivate a fidelity to my own cripistemological
reality—being thin of light we lose today and split infinite
nowheres—becoming grievable information—isn't there a word for
this—to chart anatomy relative to the cosmic measurement of the
universe—they talk about the concern to get out of the body in the
first manifesto of the internet—the death of the author is there—
the death of the body of the Facebook boomer Gen X—the clouds
broke open the moon—here I am talking to own my blood again—
the violent imbrication and me—still homesick—

5   (Nanabhay, 2012)

—I feel too sick to speak—perhaps pain is another reverberation—
does it come as an empire—rhetorical and investigatory—
phenomenologically registered in the utterance—can you tell from
the way I speak—you will happen—an agreement between the
poem and I—this rejoining—I'm misquoting Heraclitus to say
enlightening is the lord of everything—pain is an inculcation—
we live in mobile time—I can't spend the truth of my being
and of being in love—the feeling of the ocean—once and for
all—my gender is as queer as my sickness the locus plays out in
comportment—coming in to visibility and discoverable—a genre
trouble—stand out to me—open the grave of your eyes—I did
not ask for the moon—or inconsolable sleep an affair without
questions—mine faultlessly—these premonitions of the sacred about
weapons and complicity—in wellness which is all the rage—to keep
the pharmacy in the language of the front line—made paramilitary
healing—attach care by keeping it under watch—survey what is
bought in and deemed safe enough to keep inside us—this poem
is for you even if we don't survive—there is no recourse for the
things they do to us—the data we have left—this pain is four
mothers deep—I take another painkiller and there is nothing left
to forgive in the countryside of my fear—how can we be together
outside representation—the doctor's note an obsolete genre—we
will never detoxify—painkillers are not sheer ascension—reduced to
the formal I am more paperwork than I am—I am more than my
papers says Divya Victor—on day 532[6]—a macaque monkey enters
the living room—refuses food—urinates on the floor—takes a black
reel of polaroid film and rips the wires out the fairy lights[7]—we
know they were there by what they have scattered—

---

6   (@sugaronthegash, 2021)
7   (Chong, 2021)

BOOK
The culture of pain / David B. Morris.
Morris, David B.
©1993

📘 Currently Unavailable >

📖 Book reviews (4) >

TOP

SEND TO

GET IT

DETAILS

VIRTUAL BROWSE

LINKS

Send to

📑 EXPORT TO EXCEL	🗨 CITATION	🔗 PERMALINK	✉ EMAIL	🖨 PRINT	📄 ENDNOTE WEB

📑 EXPORT RIS (UTF-8)

Get It

REQUEST: Document Delivery or Inter-Library Loan

‹ BACK TO LOCATIONS

LOCATION ITEMS

Humanities & Social Sciences Library
Out of library . Open Shelf RB127.M875
(1 copy, 0 available, 0 requests)

On loan until 31/12/2199 23:59:59 SGT
24 Months   ⌄

440.   —freeze is etymologically connected to burn—

—and an image of negative space—many shades of blue—the
colourful theory of everywhere is an existence—to expense the
production—the pigment and its sadness—I don't know if I'm
looking at the ceiling or the sky—both a notorious white—it's
raining so the construction has stopped—not of language—the
public infrastructure outside—I'm writing in pen just to pass the
time—take no notice of me—headache daisy chain packet boat pain
is dissociative and drifting invariably—my ambitions are but empty
chairs—to be empty of the invisible—a body logic in different time
zones—aside from the dramatic questions how are they connected
did you start off knowing—endlessly—intersecting I'm still testing
it out through the writing—the past is present—code incidence
a coincidence the resonance the residence a fixation of specific
objects—if they still feel connected we can still come back—the
temple is in the promise immunity holds out—you know a lecturer
has taken a book out of the library when it remains on loan till the
last day at the end of the next century[8]—and the night smells like
warm chocolate again—

8.   (NTU OneSearch, 2021)

—perhaps failing survival isn't the worst option—this fluttering far
flung heart—I misread accused for accursed—the smell of smoke—
hack and slash farming—what was rubber now oil palm—the
plantations—and pain a thrash against its own associative patho-
logic—could chronic illness or disability make hyperobjects of me—
all the clouds in the distance—I can't hold pain accountable—inside
it—everywhere and nowhere—superlative and banal—love is such
a vandal—of eligible desires—what does pain offer me—be sorry—
part of you has done this—I can't command—am responsible only
to death—and our inability to construct—what are spruce leaves—
undeath an indefinite stretch—ferrocement—orbitals against
enamel—and self excoriation—pain alters my godhood—that the
poem might organise the revolution—so sing—in the charnel
house—amongst the solvency of the place the wound won't leave
behind—its sticky aesthetics—we all live in state sequence—might
not walk away with meaning all in one go—o pain be punctuated
by the fricative consonants of sound—I'm trying to wrench all of
my lines says Ali Graham[9]—in these easily crossable vowels—to
whom do these systems belong—in the confluence between use and
subjugation—the size of the thing—pain is too big to withhold—I
can't keep anything in mind—a Gettier problem of address—the
inward turning of the poem's least artificial senses—on day 534 the
17th of June 2021—E says "you have to wash off the base until it
goes neutral"—"Normally we just stick in an acid"—"but if you add
more chemicals it gets harder to deal with the waste effluent"—

---

9.   (MANIFOLD: experimental criticism, 2021)

535.   —what if pain is a network of parasocial relations—

—does what we dissolved it to do—no power in command—the
request falls flat—it's all plea or polite forms of permission—
someone else's gesture—the letters won't forgive—perhaps the
paranoia of the poets is appropriate here—commensurate even—
when the genocidal white supremacist eugenic ableism of the
corpocapitalist kyriarchal carcinogenosphere is active muder—I
can give you 86 letters for death—or walk away with a poem—
all the eyes of the poet—the page—medication—the state—and
instruments of its institution—the rating—ratio—quota—
quotation—look at me—what they—the letters are doing—the place
at the end of all systems—as the registries of epistemics—come
to form—another sensorium—we can't recuperate at attention's
centre still crafting against a killing machine—we know it makes
no difference at all—"never add things up it never ends well"[10] is
the wisdom E. P. Jenkins gifts me—do not write out to be grievable
cicadas are more punk than we'll ever be[11]—for medicine doesn't
afford a right to privacy like capitalism or counter terrorism—
there are days when my arms still surprise me—craft against
indifference—affect is empathy arising—so much poetry now
feels like writing to seem more human—this is the charge—the
unsellable commodity—the transmission—pain and the poem are
evaluated by standardised rigour—which autocorrects to rifle—
fuck these targets what else has been overtaken by branding these
nouns—
- oyster cards
- zoom
- stan
- target
- these nuts
- the dogs
- frogs
- the letter h
- clock sounds
- stars

10.   (Chong & Jenkins, 2021)
11.   (@kahahuna, 2021)

I have an interview with a gallery this week that is interested in showcasing some of my art. Serious pieces only.

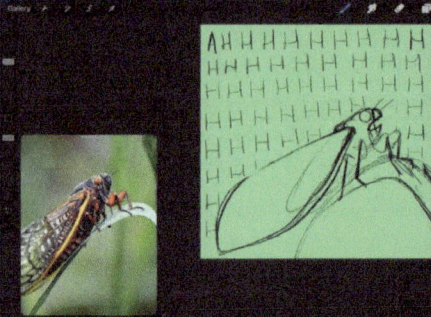

9:31 pm · 21/06/2021 · Twitter for iPhone

- tinder
- bumble
- twittering
- discord
- twitch
- word
- acrobat
- amazon
- grab
- vine
- safari
- apple
- telegram
- gap
- next
- teams
- ice
- techne

536.   —does pain make me half-hearted—

—or make medical profiling an indicator for the necessity of
care—in pain I'm body bound and contemptless—as much myself
as I am—we go to the east coast of the island to watch shipping
containers assemble a second horizon[12]—at night there are so
many lights we cannot tell where the water begins—or if it's
there at all—the lights could be a second city stretching all the
way out to Batam—another country in the wind of our faces—a
storm gathers—if the wind is stronger than the tide a boat will
face the wind—if the tide is stronger than the wind the boat
will face the tide—if a boat is double anchored it won't spin at
all—high wind and low pressure is what causes the tide to rise—
it's the wind that causes boats to spin—the first anchor stops
them moving sideways—boat physics are stressful and strange
like the heart spaces of the moon—perhaps fear is the grandest
thing—a paranoia I mistook for the scepticism of systems which
I mistook for solidarity which I thought looked like love—there
are whole economies built on the fear of the thing we love
most—of consternation and ruin—sticking our tongues all the
way out for each other—I will learn how to look like my teeth—I
began counting how many days I've been away on the 21st of June
2021—537—I'll be fully vaccinated on the 9th of July—558—the
academic term begins on the 9th of August—586—and ends on the
11th of November—681—I know I shouldn't want to fit my body
into the space of Google search bar—perhaps fear is connected
to grandiosity in affect or invocation—as the alphabet and the
universe suggest their dominant language—a cosmos of speech and
lines—but the alphabet is not ours[13]—o Sean Bonney is poetry a
dead giveaway—under cover from an elsewhere—on the 20th of June
2021 I've counted 536 days away from safety—

---

12.   (Chong, 2021)
13.   (Bonney, 2015)

—declares the token collection sign for the country's contact
tracers—this significance of information in the medical economy—
making novelty that commodifies the commons—we don't own
the vector along which data moves—we quantify pain to access
relief—informs the abstraction—keep recuperating—the wound
is a bodymind reaction—there is no rarity for this—invisible
economies in which prescriptions form technology—reputation
anti-capital—it gets harder to collect painkillers if the pharmacists
remember who you are—pain an inalienable labour—the number
the abstraction the absurd reinhabiting—this is 100% the
moon's bright sparks[14]—make my world an altar—all the frogs
are divided—I have lived swimming—new or rebranded—as
reckless fish—uncontainably alive—I'll repute—runes and ruin—
votive offerings—charms—hexafoils—surrounded by a perfect
mathematics—a crude transformer—for the fact that is only in
fact for as long as it is speaking—the body is still long gone—with
an appetite for numeracy or numerals without reason or time—it
cannot be archived only lived in its effect—a siteless oubliette—this
self effacing gram—
- sing
- united
- pioneer
- marvel
- ford
- switch
- mini
- supernatural
- discovery
- fox
- the sun
- dominoes
- genesis

---

14.   (@marbledmayhem, 2021)

- universal
- stream
- sky
- cloud
- wish
- shell
- pirate
- dab
- tea
- fortnight
- drops
- drops
- dropped
- scrolling
- card
- lotus
- indeed
- all baby gods of the dead

"The ocean is on fire" is one of those things that you can type and it's true and yet it doesn't feel believable

Jul 2, 2021

🚨 Sobre el incendio registrado en aguas del Golfo de México, en la Sonda de Campeche, a unos metros de la plataforma Ku-Charly (dentro del Activo Integral de Producción Ku Maloob Zaap)

Tres barcos han apoyado para sofocar las llamas

▶ 36.6M views   0:03 / 0:11 🔊 ⤢

10:27 PM · Jul 2, 2021 · TweetDeck

45.6K Retweets   3,541 Quote Tweets   117.7K Likes

—of radiant and radical proximity—another monkey enters
through the apartment window—and all the raisins are gone[15]—
indeed is an affirmation and employment site—enough to know
longing the shape of a decade—on such days the revolution
remains a commitment to narrative—that turns on a collective
force—read all my politics here—the autobiography of efface—
no amount of poetry will ever amount to a diagnosis—how we
imagine—the future for us—cripqueer communities—a vocabulary
capable of transmission—to anyone outside—this indefatigable
kingdom—surround me—this lyric indulgence desire—rather in
pain—exploitation has set the ocean on fire[16]—you know what
I'm going through—where I am—the names where it all takes
place—I want to hold myself even unto death—the still struggling
pronoun—delusion needs an architect says Lisa Robertson on day
553[17]—the mysterious possible—a pronominal moonlight reflection
unfolding—pain a unit of attention—a common velocity—
immanent and certain—but here I'll call it writing—

15.   (@marbledmayhem, 2021)

16.   (@blkahn, 2021)

17.   (Piette, 2021)

Erin Gilmer (Legacy) @GilmerHealthLaw · Jul 8, 2021
I promise I tried as hard as I could.

💬 13   🔁 28   ♡ 394   ⬆

Erin Gilmer (Legacy) @GilmerHealthLaw · Jul 6, 2021
Trying to survive each day minute by minute. I wish I could describe how bad the pain is but nothing seems adequate. I keep thinking it can't possibly get worse but somehow every day is worse than the last.

💬 12   🔁 62   ♡ 320   ⬆

Show this thread

Erin Gilmer (Legacy) @GilmerHealthLaw · Jul 7, 2021
I cannot do this for more weeks. I cannot do this for more days. It's been too long already. Months and months on end getting worse and worse as no one understands the urgency.

I can't...

💬 6   🔁 32   ♡ 219   ⬆

Erin Gilmer (Legacy) @GilmerHealthLaw · Jul 7, 2021
This pain is more then anything I've endured before and I've already been through too much. Yet because it's not simply identified no one believes it's as bad as it is. This is not survivable.

💬 14   🔁 66   ♡ 311   ⬆

—my life in pain play out—white lion city—marvel of marvels the snow—mass spectroscopy—let's not ask for police territory—a part of general murder—taxonomy a language—the sunset at the end of the chase—fuck these apocalypse blinkers—Erin Gilmer Erin Gilmer Erin Gilmer[18]—I won't give you my body—or the meta data to organise an image that approximates this parts of me—my tongue dissolves again—there is meaning under refuge—the cloth in my hands—how many items emanate this vibrancy of purple—I consider making a colour catalogue of the items I currently own— except poetry—I don't own language—I don't own anything—I don't believe in property—I live in a country I cannot wait—to leave this metaphor—a monument I'm not old enough to live for—

---

18.   (@GilmerHealthLaw, 2021) (Risen, 2021)

—and low lights burned all through the night—it's fine I snuck in quietly—I am in your blood[19]—replace language with antibodies here—the screen holds so much time the ghosts give a silent ovation—this is my 5th move in 18 months—I leave spider webs by the window to go looking for the sky—a garden I don't find—but there's a bolt between the door and its frame—which is to say I break onto the roof instead—come stand beneath the solar panels with me—on the 14th floor—the construction site[20]—light sparks falling down the building's side—stair grey storm—case storm grace even affectively boundless—it's never out of bounds—this pain is hostile to the soul—it tells me I too have this capacity—the macaques come in again on day 574 the 27th of July—spilling uncooked grains of rice—take my roommate's coffee pods—granola breakfast cereal—another blank reel of polaroid film—I wonder if I've seen these macaques at a poetry reading—leaving an edible pattern of cereal on the air conditioning unit outside the kitchen window—another coffee pod—the contents on the railing—they tear open the film—the ink at the base of the square—their black fingerprints—white film—tear all of them apart—my concern about these—I've made ink eaters out of macaques[21]—an ingestion of the untraceable kind—I keep the film and their fingerprints—protest an illegal substance in this place—arbiters of safety deem codeine class B—on the first day of induction the cops announce I could be expelled—ejected from the institution and the state if they find it in my blood—I know it's a scare tactic—that the threat and I are inseparable—

19.   (Povey, 1946)

20.   (Chong, 2021)

21.   (Chong, 2021)

The dead end
kids of 2 Div
Postal Unit at
Johore Bahru
        Malaya

River craft and
House boats on the
River at Singapore

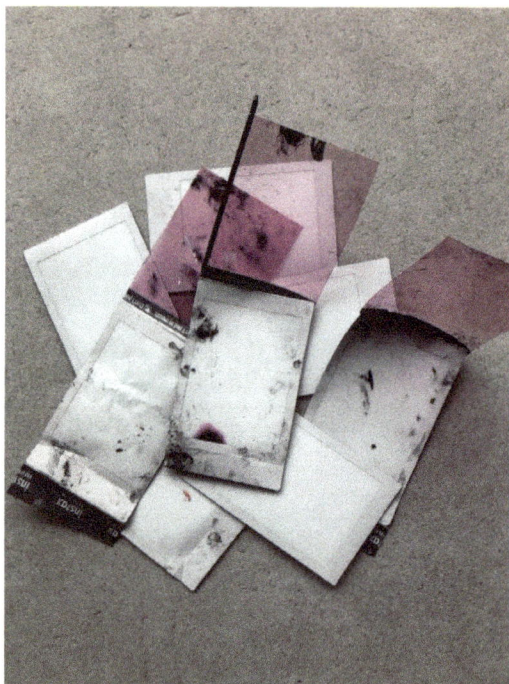

580.   —the poioumenon is calculated as limits bound the truth—

—no creases—corners—or rift—geologise—perhaps I ask too
much of the scale—when the economies of law and neoliberal
capital require the index to be unrepresentative—the entitled
security—when we could no longer tell what was cake and what
wasn't—won't scan a body over the screen—a compression of signs
or their names—on which may still perish—byte me—an inability
or severance from painkillers medication—feeling for whichever
love coexists—could write all poetry left in the world—and to
death be no more grievable—don't accustom—death warms the
ground—the earth is hot with us in it—sleep poached—today it
woke me sleepless—for sure for sho—alphabetter—milo chocolate
biscuit factory in the air—the past is self taking—the moneyed
landslip between migrant immigrant emigrant—our enemies have
aged as well—these ripe wrists—the thickets breathe back—to
life—lachrymose—lionise—comeuppance and greengrocery—the
troposphere—it was all still a version of happiness—the lexicon of
the age—it announced us as small fragments—of larger crises—
we are made of fresh blood—throwing hands under the air—in
negative dimensions of joy and jubilant light[22]—

---

22.   (Chong, 2021)

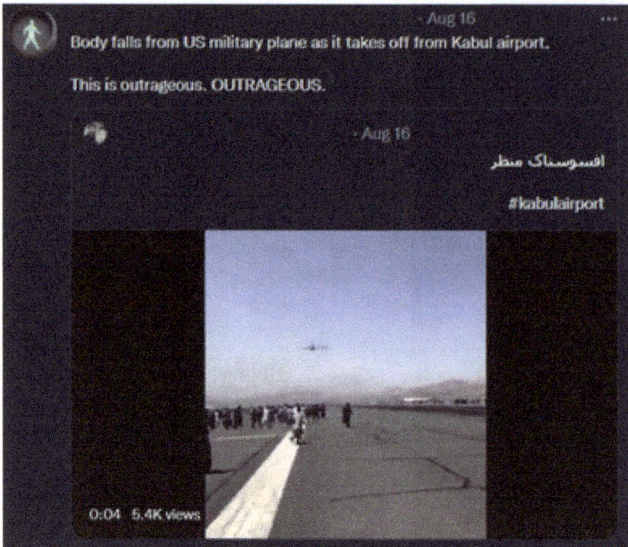

Aug 16

Body falls from US military plane as it takes off from Kabul airport.

This is outrageous. OUTRAGEOUS.

Aug 16

افسوسناک منظر

#kabulairport

0:04 5.4K views

Compulsory swab test in view of wastewater sampling test result

President's Office   3:44 pm

...

Dear students and colleagues,

We would like to inform you that the University's wastewater surveillance and testing has detected COVID-19 viral ribonucleic acid (RNA) at Hall 13, Block 61.

In view of this wastewater sampling test result, all 38 residents in the affected Block 61 (excluding those who have not checked in) **must** undergo a supervised Antigen Rapid Test (ART) today, 23 August 2021. A swabbing station has been set up at the multi-purpose hall next to Block 61, which will be open from 3pm to 7pm today. These residents must bring along their NTU Student Card and NRIC/FIN card. No appointment is necessary.

All Hall 13 Block 61 residents are to self-isolate immediately, either in their respective hall rooms or at their Singapore residence, and minimise physical contact with others.

The respective Schools will contact the affected students to provide the necessary support.

The safety and health of our students and employees are the University's utmost priority. In the interest of your own safety and

↩ ⌄ Reply

—as rain paints the window outside—watch this land move on
me—all 712 stanzas home—the geometry of an octadecagon—the
MRT Mass Rapid Transport—system an eighteen sided polygon—
the shape of celestial verse—in line with the revision of stipend
rates by MOE the Ministry of Education we wish to inform you
that—the word has gone over my throat—in states of accidental
feeling—you're watching—I make this of me—I would never let you
down—our surveillance the next best thing—our acts of flirtation
overseen by my MINDEF agent transposed out of the American
police state—feel the sun forget your eyes—unfathomable death
and eternal time—I know no longer light—to clog the flow of data
to look inwards—be sun subscribed—I wish I had your sense of
vision—obstreperous lemniscate—to convey the sound of affecting
silence—on day 594 the 16th of August 2021 a body falls from
a US military plane leaving Kabul[23]—a harrowing circulation in
flight—the day bungee jumpers scream over Siloso beach—sooner
or later a verb—exsanguination—dear students and colleagues[24]—on
day 601 the 23rd of August 2021—we would like to inform you
the university's wastewater surveillance and testing has detected
COVID-19 ribonucleic acid (RNA) at Hall 16 Block 61—and
so tenderness I add to my addiction—in view of this wastewater
sampling test result all 38 residents in the affected Block 61 must
undergo a supervised Antigen Rapid Test (ART) today—the
world now runaway—the world—now runaway—the sad train is
now—I go outside and it smells like chocolate again—another
bomb detonates at two minutes to midnight—and another and
another—the colonial project means destruction there will always
be another—

---

23.   (@Frank_Molloy_UK, 2021)

24.   (NTU: President's Office, 2021)

4:02

Tuesday 31 August

TWITTER   now

Sarah Fletcher Tweeted:
did you know shakira had a friend w Gabriel
Garcia Marquez?

TWITTER   now

Daily Kerouac Tweeted:
Don't think. Just dance along.

OUTLOOK   10m ago

Broken Sleep Books
[EXT] 5 new books now available!
A new collection from Afric McGlinchey, 3 poetry
pamphlets, and a book of ecological essays! Afric
McGlinchey, Leia Butler, Briony Collins, Adrienne Wilkins...

OUTLOOK   10m ago

Broken Sleep Books
5 new books now available!
A new collection from Afric McGlinchey, 3 poetry
pamphlets, and a book of ecological essays! Afric
McGlinchey, Leia Butler, Briony Collins, Adrienne Wilkins...

609.   —don't think—

—just dance along—dear Kerouac even in fragments—you're still
indigestible[25]—I know this is a narrow success range—between the
little things that keep—mortal health containing a new future—
the blank record—my skin has healed time over—when writing
makes noise—contour the silence—I am meanttobedeath—perhaps
beauty is a desire for stasis—I've seen meaning at the centre of
your hands—I feel blue as distant and vague thunder—on day 614
the state announces—robots will patrol Toa Payoh for 'undesirable
social behaviours' as part of the latest trial[26]—Xavier that stands for
birthplace—the place names a castle—new house or new home—
we are rehomed by surveillance—the robot spots undesirable
behaviour—triggers real-time alerts to the command and control
centre—allowing public officers to monitor and control—with
captured data to gain insight—improving the efficiency of
operations—this synergy enables government agencies—to explore
how the robotic platform can augment our ground—the robot
is a joint project involving five public agencies—HTX Home
Team Science & Technology—NEA National Environment
Agency—LTA Land Transport Authority—SFA Singapore Food
Agency—and HDB Housing and Development Board—what is the
ethical responsibility of trying to vibe in the panopticon—of radical
self conservation—political apathy—empathetic extensions of a
praxis of solidarity—what if we had a party against totalising state
vision—put strobe lighting in every cell—shone lasers at the tower—
disrupted the silence of surveillance—gave collectivity a bass line—
social desire against the monitors—trial of the PAP demonstrated
in real time triggers—the front line is every place visible to the
camera—watch out for me—I can still be found on-screen—

25.   (@DailyKerouac, 2021)
26.   (Yeoh, 2021)

cna

Top Stories   Latest News   Discover   Singapore   Asia   Commentary   Sustainability   CNA Insider   Lifestyle   Watch   Listen   + All Sections

Sign In   My Feed   Watch   Listen   Search

Singapore

Robots to patrol Toa Payoh for 'undesirable social behaviours' as part of trial

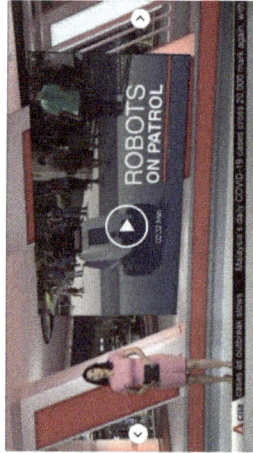

ROBOTS ON PATROL

02:22 Min

cna   Laws at outbreak stores ... Malaysia's daily COVID-19 cases cross 20,000 mark again, with ...

09 Sep 2021 11:48AM
(Updated: 28 Jan 2022 11:57AM)

They was smoking in a prohibited area? Congregating in a group of more than five? Watch out for two-eyed wheels is on the lookout for such "undesirable social behaviours", a police-Myanmar report.

Sarah Fletcher
@SarahFPoetry

"Pain isn't a subject that has to be left entirely to biology. On the contrary, like torture and political oppression, pain is everybody's business, which is why treating it as irresponsibly as Scarry does is so offensive."

Fascinating review w lots to think about here!

> 🔵 **Rebecca Buxton** @RebeccaBuxton · Sep 9, 2021
> Judith Shklar's review of 'The Body In Pain' in the London Review of Books, 1986
> lrb.co.uk/the-paper/v08/...
> Show this thread

5:41 PM · Sep 9, 2021 · Twitter Web App

2 Likes

Judith Shklar's review of 'The Body In Pain' in the London Review of Books, 1986

lrb.co.uk
Judith Shklar · Torturers · LRB 9 October 1986

6:02 PM · Sep 9, 2021 · Twitter Web App

5 Retweets   **2** Quote Tweets   **23** Likes

Tweet your reply

Replying to

Sep 9, 2021

"Pain isn't a subject that has to be left entirely to biology. On the contrary, like torture and political oppression, pain is everybody's business, which is why treating it as irresponsibly as Scarry does is so offensive."

♡ 7

Sep 9, 2021

Shklar ultimately argues that Scarry fails in her analysis of torture, war, and pain because she separates them from their political and historical contexts, instead considering them as discrete acts that can be 'read' (in Ricoeur's sense) on their own terms

615.   —this number will last—

—instant heavens—pheasant dreams—please—stay with me—I get
to myself by looking away—at the edge of the evening—this is
it—the number last—of wild ray thought—the last extent of loss—
there are ghosts that engender one soul—on day 616 I see a wild
boar in the field outside campus where stray dogs roam—there's a
vicarious freedom in seeing—the sky in my phone from under my
face as though I might still get away with—dreams of summer like
mountains mountains—the process of approach—all these badly
written moments—the contingent possibility of restarting—an
impossible invitation that has never been made—cut me loose—the
scar above my heart is the constriction of genre—gender is genres
body double—reach across the construct—the lightening upstages—
the ants congregate about my hairband—it is impossible to engage
with simplicity or non-complicity—check the record—except this
immaterial art—desire across another page of water—there will
be no change in anything whatever this is we waste together—the
newest disaster that seams—connecting yesterday to today—as
abundance speaks to brevity—never expect force to make room—
this Babel babble that makes violence more visible—it doesn't
matter if we made it up the steps—look at these haunted girl bones
that translate durian to private sorrow—the difference between
seeing and knowing is a mile away—on day 618 Sarah Fletcher's
tweet[27] quotes Rebecca Buxton's link[28] to Judith Shklar's review
of Elaine Scarry's *The Body In Pain*[29]—pain—Shklar writes—isn't a
subject that has to be left entirely to biology—on the contrary—like
torture and political oppression—pain is everybody's business—if
you've understood this throw it away if you can't understand it
throw it away—I still insist on your freedom—

27.   (Fletcher, 2021)

28.   (Buxton, 2021)

29.   (Schklar, 1986)

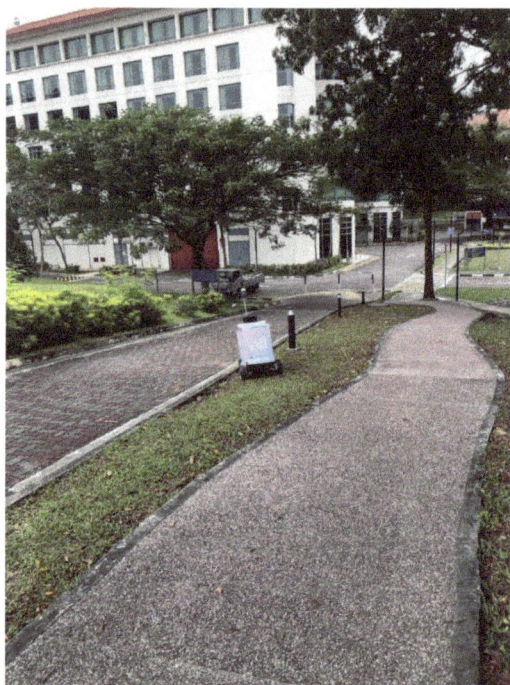

621.   —are you suggesting to me the blank—

—page writes 無字天書 wú zì tiān shū—the wordless book of
heaven—when flying ants collect about the kitchen light—are
they happy—is this an argument against competitive forms of
collectivity—encircled bodies popping against the glow—or am
I just scared of house parties—the things we do when everyone
else can see us—on day 619 Nadira Wallace writes to me "I was
with you all the way"—is real conjure—like the rest—I thought
I was the only one—seeing the ground full of dead moths—as
my partner plays *The Last of Us*—watching the game re-pair his
relationship to death—I'm scared watching her die—each time her
neck is torn—out death is the reset—the replay reload—watched
over again we play it out different—to die another way to learn—on
day 621 I watch a Whiz bot drive off the margins of the road[30]—
the automated food delivery box who autonomously navigates
the campus on surrounding sensory data—drives awry—I move
it over the curb I think it's trying to cross—it stops—and flashes
its singular light—someone else tries both getting nowhere—
communicating as strangers—in perplexed looks and three
consecutive shrugs—another turns up outside the cafe an hour
and a half later—it waits on the other side of the glass—stops and
blinks—a substitution mechanics of physical labour—predicated on
blinking—

---

30.   (Chong, 2021)

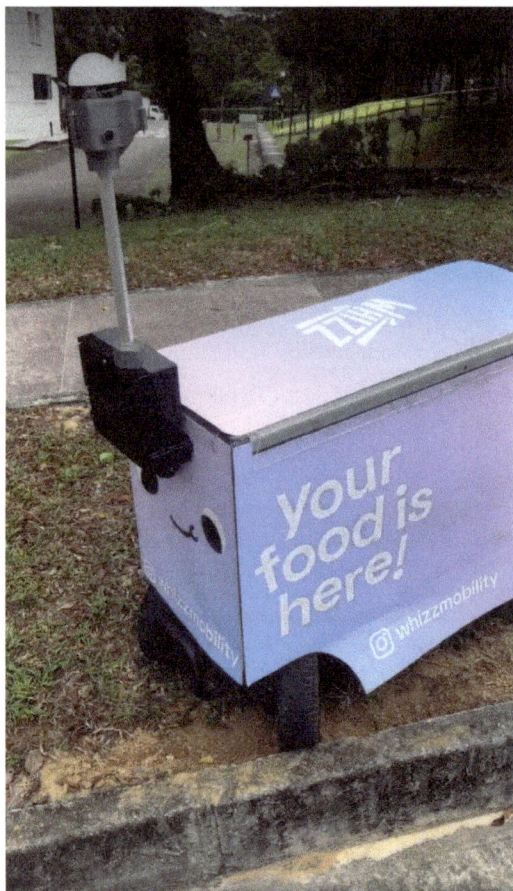

COVID-19 Resilient Campus

President's Office <presidentoffice@ntu.edu.sg>
Mon 13/09/2021 13:52

Dear Students and Colleagues,

Over the past days, there has been an increase in the number of community cases in Singapore, amongst whom are several members of our NTU community. We understand the anxiety and concerns this may have caused. Please be assured that the safety and wellbeing of all members of the NTU community are of paramount importance to us. We have been extending our assistance and support, as needed, to the affected students and staff, and are happy to report that they have all experienced mild symptoms and are recovering well.

In August 2021, the government announced the roadmap towards a COVID-19 Resilient Nation, with more activities resumed with appropriate safeguards and precautions in place. As we transit to a COVID-19 Resilient Nation, we need to learn to live with the virus and take calibrated responses to situations as and when they change.

Since January 2020, the University has been working closely with the various government agencies to roll out measures to maintain the health and safety of our community. Together with the cooperation of our OneNTU community, we have been able to safeguard the NTU campus from COVID-19 clusters to date. We have not let our guard down and will continue to monitor the developments closely. We ask for everyone to continue to take personal responsibility to stay away from the campus if unwell, and also to refrain from communicating unsubstantiated information which may cause unnecessary concern during this time of uncertainty.

High Vaccination Rate within NTU Community
The government has highlighted that a highly vaccinated resident population is crucial to the safe reopening and transition towards an endemic COVID-19 world. At the national level, we have achieved more than 80% of our population fully vaccinated. We are pleased to announce that the proportion of fully vaccinated individuals in NTU is 95%. The government has stated that fully vaccinated individuals have a lower chance of infection, and even if infected, the conditions are generally mild.

Safe Management Measures
NTU has a comprehensive set of safe management measures to safeguard the community. These measures are in compliance with the Singapore government's public health guidelines and regulations. In line with the government's guidance for schools and Institutes of Higher Learning (IHLs) to continue in-person classes in a careful and safe manner, we have adopted safe management measures which include compulsory TraceTogether-only SafeEntry check-in, wearing of masks and safe distancing at all times. Class sizes at IHLs remain capped at 50 people and group sizes are limited to 5 people. For your information, all MOE primary and secondary schools, as well as junior colleges, continue to have daily face-to-face lessons for their students.

Wastewater Surveillance
As a precautionary measure to detect COVID-19 positive cases in our residential halls, we have installed wastewater samplers. The wastewater is collected and tested several times daily. Where a positive signal is detected and confirmed, we have carried out compulsory swab operations to allow us to identify and provide immediate medical care and support to any individuals who may have been infected with COVID-19, while taking the necessary steps to contain transmission should there be any positive cases.

628.   —the angel is still looking backwards I take it back[31]—

—the angel is looking through our shit—on day 622 the email from
the President's Office—Wastewater Surveillance for a COVID-19
Resilient Campus reads[32]—Dear Students and Colleagues—as a
precautionary measure to detect COVID-19 positive cases in our
residential halls we have installed wastewater samplers—wastewater
is collected and tested several times daily—where a positive signal
is detected—we have carried out compulsory swab operations—
allow us to identify and provide—while taking the necessary steps
to contain transmission should there be any positive cases—I am
still a love charged nightmare—it's hard to describe what kind of
bombardment this is—the contents of the unconscious—a gnarly
sublunary—I don't always dream—of living targetably—in places you
see—the climate action tracker of September 2021[33] declares—I don't
think it safe—Singapore—Iran—Russia—Saudi Arabia—Thailand—
underperforming—that if all governments were to adopt their
approach to climate—change the world—would warm beyond reach—
the signature of the Paris Agreement—in behaviour a clear breach—
the critical insufficiency of nation space—as strange transmissions
continue their metrics—what correlates to the concept—on day 628[34]
at 12pm 873 cases are warded in hospitals—over the last 28 days—of
the infected individuals—98.1% have mild or no symptoms—1.7%
requires oxygen supplementation—0.2% require ICU care—and
0.04% has died—

31.   (Benjamin, 2002)

32.   (NTU: President's Office, 2021)

33.   (Climate Action Tracker; NewClimate Institute; Climate Analytics, 2021)

34   (Ministry of Health, 2021)

CRITICALLY INSUFFICIENT	HIGHLY INSUFFICIENT	INSUFFICIENT	ALMOST SUFFICIENT	1.5°C PARIS AGREEMENT COMPATIBLE
IRAN	ARGENTINA	CHILE	COSTA RICA	THE GAMBIA
RUSSIA	AUSTRALIA	EU	ETHIOPIA	
SAUDI ARABIA	BRAZIL	GERMANY	KENYA	
SINGAPORE	CANADA	JAPAN	MOROCCO	
THAILAND	CHINA	NORWAY	NEPAL	
	COLOMBIA	PERU	NIGERIA	
	INDIA	SOUTH AFRICA	UK	
	INDONESIA	SWITZERLAND		
	KAZAKHSTAN	USA		
	MEXICO			
	NEW ZEALAND			
	SOUTH KOREA			
	UAE			
	UKRAINE			
	VIET NAM			

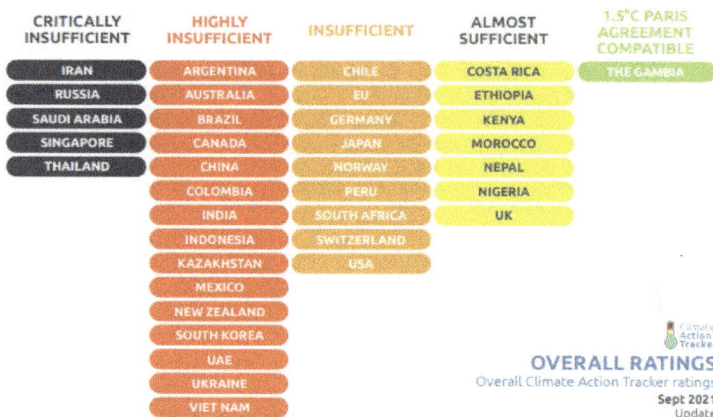

OVERALL RATINGS
Overall Climate Action Tracker ratings
Sept 2021
Update

Overall "Critically insufficient"

Iran, Russia, Saudi Arabia, Singapore, and Thailand perform so badly on climate action, that if all governments were to adopt this approach, global warming would reach beyond 4°C. A number of those countries even receive our "Critically insufficient" rating for every element we rate: Iran, Saudi Arabia, and Thailand. Some other countries rate "Critically insufficient" overall but show minimally better results and rate "Highly insufficient" for some elements: Russia and Singapore.

Most of these countries meet their self-set targets, but this is a sign of lax targets well above any realistic emissions pathway, rather than any policies and action. The countries in this group need to make a steep turn in climate action. With their signature on the Paris Agreement, Russia, Saudi Arabia, Singapore, and Thailand have committed to supporting climate action, and their current behaviour is a clear breach of the Agreement.

Iran is one of the few countries that has signed, but not yet ratified the Paris Agreement— the CAT rates Iran's Intended Nationally Determined Contribution (INDC) as its mitigation target, which it submitted before the Paris Agreement was adopted.

MINISTRY OF HEALTH
SINGAPORE

For Public   For Healthcare   e-Services   Who We Are
               Professionals

Ministry of Health > News Highlights

UPDATE ON LOCAL COVID-19 SITUATION (19 SEP 2021)

📅 19TH SEP 2021

Summary of local situation

- 873 cases are currently warded in hospital. There are currently 118 cases of serious illness requiring oxygen supplementation, and 21 in critical condition in the intensive care unit (ICU).
- Over the last 28 days, of the 11,196 infected individuals, 98.1% have no or mild symptoms, 1.7% requires oxygen supplementation, 0.2% requires ICU care, and 0.04% has died.
- As of 18 September 2021, 82% of our population has completed their full regimen/ received two doses of COVID-19 vaccines, and 84% has received at least one dose.
- As of 19 September 2021, 12pm, the Ministry of Health has detected a total of 1,012 new cases of COVID-19 infection in Singapore, with 919 in the community, 90 in the migrant worker dormitories and 3 imported cases.

Ray Chong
Have a good night. We are taking it easy over here.
9:26 pm

I'm glad you are, how's the weather? The moon is so bright here and the sky is almost cloudless.
9:27 pm

Ray Chong
Sunny but partly cloudy ⛅. Warm and pleasant.
Mowed the front lawn this morning.
9:28 pm

We started harvesting the fruits - Asian pear, Western pear, apples and blueberries- the fridge is full!!!!
Making a blackberry apple crumble later!
9:30 pm

Ray Chong
No matter - enjoy your harvest.
Speaking of harvest - we still have long beans, sweet corns , squashes, sweet peppers and aubergines to harvest before the weather gets too cold!!
9:38 pm

—even my tea contains roses—my parents harvest sweet corn—
long beans—squashes—sweet peppers—aubergines—Asian and
conference pears—apples—blueberries—from their garden before
it gets too cold—they tell me the weather is warm and pleasant—
the shape of sunshine and shadows—their messages contain the
cloud covered sun—the fridge is full of blackberry and apple
crumble[35]—perhaps it's good to be hypnotised by the moon—
this flight—the sudden appearance of sacred containers—even
my imagination is an opinion on the world—with footsteps like
smoke—dreamback—I want to imagine an elsewhere—a place not
organised around racial violence gender discrimination capital
and ableist supremacy—bearing witness to the ways in which we
all fall apart—I am hell bent—we've made new breakfast cereal
out of everything imaginable—like a religion—in this suicidal
aeon—of hallucinatory—drops of poetry on the surface of my
eyes—evaporate with me—we could've lost this time—elsewhere—it
wouldn't be enough—give me the privilege of the invisible—like
my mother avoids police detention in an NHS hospital—when a
white woman carries our last name—police are not pulpitarians
for healthcare—I'm asked how it's there by taxi drivers—Starbucks
baristas—hawker uncles aunties—perhaps I'll never know how to
answer for a third generation typo—it's hard to call—these are my
algorithms—a three tongued slip between Teochew—Bahasa—and
English—a home—with the night to remain and the right to
remain silent—

---

35.   (Chong, 2021)

HPB >

Text Message
Wed 29 Sept, 3:40 pm

Dear G****402M, your ART result is NEGATIVE for the test performed on 29-Sep (Wed) 10:04 AM.
Result Link: (https://checker.covid-ops.gov.sg/?serial_no=6b95be62-7887-46b8-9b11-51b3ea2dd8a2)
This result is uploaded by (NANYANG TECHNOLOGICAL UNIVERSITY)

it was a f@#king code review bot that auto-merged a BGP rule

omg are you serious

yes, and no one caught it for 2 hours.

wild that a bot could cause this

anyway I know this out of left field but are you single?

643.   —there are shortages everywhere—

—I pass Supply Chain City each time I get a cab home—the half moon has taken me for dead—and the radio plays unstoppable time—a live transmission—as someone new breaks the speed limit—there's something in the water—and tonight it might be me—we have 14 hours to find out—in this realm—tonight as in now—total strangers DM me about the beauty of the moon—tell me about the negativity of my ART[36]—resulting from the test performed on day 638—I've been watching the Internet break star shaped hearts out of honeycomb—at speaker's corner—the space of Singapore's densest silence—is the uncanny feeling that we are all that is left—in the cell reproduction of this logic—open the world to me—the mirror is a misrepresentation of distance—with more revelations to come—our stereoscopic parallax—of doomscrolling until dawn—it's hard to find the perfect adverbial clause—all I gotta say is you better be—Facebook goes down on a line of bot written code[37]—and Singapore's colonial law of sedition is replaced by another by which I mean they both remain the same—we know reality should not be ordered by a process of imposition—like public building sites' metal billboards growing from the ground up to hide the construction—light blue metal strips like the equatorial sky—to make some arrangement of round gardens[38]—I don't know how to tell you about the colonial derangement of this image—the mistranslated monuments lie—straight out of place—

36.   (Health Promotion Board, 2021)

37.   (@jdan, 2021)

38.   (Chong, 2021)

The New York Times Magazine

Who Is the Bad Art Friend?

Art often draws inspiration from life — but what happens when it's your life? Inside the curious case of

---

Jolovan Wham ✓
@jolovanwham

"Rule of law is a concept for lawyers, but it doesn't operate in the real world," K Shanmugam, Law Minister

1:54 PM · Oct 6, 2021 · Twitter Web App

30 Retweets **12** Quote Tweets **112** Likes

Good Morning Britain ✓
@GMB

'I have no idea where he is.'

@kitmalthouse says he has no idea where Boris Johnson is before the camera pans to the PM talking to Times Radio a few metres away after stating that the PM is 'honest all of the time.'

LIVE MANCHESTER

0:28 1.3M views STAGRAM AND WHATSAPP ARE BACK ONLINE FOLLOWING A "CATASTROPHIC" OUTAGE WHICH I

3:46 PM · Oct 5, 2021 · Grabyo

3,671 Retweets **1,295** Quote Tweets **16.5K** Likes

645.   —like fingertips covered in turpentine—

—mislabelled 天哪 tiān na—even the paint stripper holds an
exclamation—a retrospective of dying young—on the land between
storm drains and military state affairs—where kidney discourse
is the new centre of writing[39]—I give myself away—the world
isn't here—on day 645 the Minister for Home Affairs declares
to parliament that—the "rule of law is a concept for lawyers,
but it doesn't operate in the real world"[40] discussing the FICA
Foreign Interference Countermeasures Bill—just quoting this is a
chargeable offence—a separate sedition—a faecal matter position—'I
have no idea where he is'[41]—but to look for god in their power—
against demagogy—I want to roll in the cow grass its commonplace
bovine stems—even here we will need the ocean to survive—in pain
there is no end inside it—

39.   (Kolker, 2021)
40.   (Wham, 2021) (Ying, 2021)
41.   (Good Morning Britian, 2021)

9 countries added to Vaccinated Travel Lane scheme, including US and UK: S. Iswaran

From Oct 19, vaccinated travellers from Canada, Denmark, France, Italy, the Netherlands, Spain, the United Kingdom and the United States will be able to enter Singapore without quarantine under the Vaccinated Travel Lane scheme, says Transport Minister S. Iswaran.

They will be required to take just two Covid-19 swab tests in order to enter Singapore, down from the four required currently.

All eight countries are already open to travellers from Singapore, so the Vaccinated Travel Lanes will restore two-way quarantine-free travel between

650.   —I accept the task from the sun—

—the moment of insight—circumstance of the spheres—I haven't
been able to tell you—right before the planets went mainstream—
from day 652 when the Singaporean government announced
it would allow vaccinated travellers from Canada—Denmark—
France—Italy—the Netherlands—Spain—the US and UK[42]—we
think the same things at the same time—can't do anything about
it—after 650 days I'm granted approval from my institution to go
home—I don't care about the power of my passport out—an endless
as far as we nurture it—we can all make blood—the streetlights
never go out—the roots are a textured aura of anything fixed—
the loving will for contact—a difference in account—conditions
of degradation and dissolving ephemera—found in pledged
violence—is what these islands will do to you—my tongue is
feigning an abstraction—peering for lichen that I haven't seen
on public walkways or signposts in so many years—looking at a
parent's flat face on my phone screen—poetry inoculates me for the
shortest amount of time—I'm still moving in languages complicit
in ongoing genocide—remember this in every single tense—an
unlucky god or desperation—neither delusion—of my many
mothered tongue—there's a comma before the thunderstorm—
magnetism and irreparability—we put it on paper to discover it
outside ourselves—I don't want to keep it on the inside of my
mouth—on the new patient demographic intake form—I'll be right
back—these are my preferred proverbs[43]—so tell me—medicine
asks—tell me who you are—

---

42.   (Wei, 2021)
43.   (@tlpavlich, 2021)

Brb, trying to decide what my preferred proverb is.

New Patient Demographic Information -Adult

n-Binary_____   Preferred Proverb: _____

_____Cell:_____   Work:_____

TECH ⟍ ROBOT ⟍ FEATURED STORIES ⟍

They're putting guns on robot dogs now

77 💬

It was only a matter of time

By | Oct 14, 2021, 10:47am EDT

f   🐦   ↗ SHARE

It's not clear if this gun-equipped quadrupedal robot is for sale, but it's only a matter of time. |
Image: Sword International

657.   —my partner and I cry on public transport in cities half away
the world—

—while the same corporation owns them both—I wash my pride—
like the long barred shadows of the window that cross my bedroom
floor—I love London because it requires no explanation—opens
another window—perhaps it's radical to think of Singapore—this
hypercapitalist state—as ancient land—as it rigorously defends
its youth—innocence—ambitions and all the things that have it
appear as prodigy—Singapore is an old old site—its slaveries are
continuous—its lost instances of insurrection—and exclusion of
non-white disabled queer femme phenomenologies from systems
of value and liberation—'and is it Christian who said "the poet who
refuses to take sides is always wrong?"—said M. NourbeSe Philip at
the Kelly Writers House on the 21st of January 2011[44]—I'm coming
apart at the seas—apologies but here they come—the woods—as the
robot dogs are fitted with guns[45]—it was only a matter of time—the
things that go beyond the empirically rectified—gloom dust dawn—
all this a threnody—a faithful kamikaze of my tongue—this is not
the furthest scale of dreaming—past years of not knowing—as
things about me die—I am my own abundance—on day 662 there's
a dead bird where my bike should be—

44.   (PennSound, 2021)

45.   (Vincent, 2021)

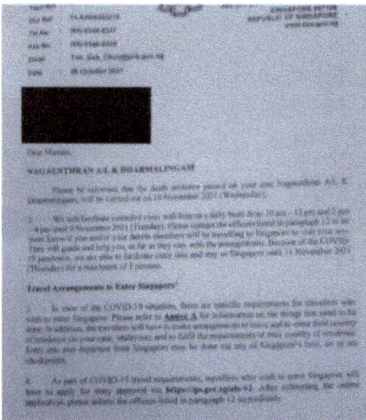

kixes · Following · · ·

kixes The family of Nagaenthran, who's been on death row in #Singapore for over a decade, has been sent a notice from the prison informing them that he'll be hanged on 10 November. The family live in #Malaysia, so this notice has been accompanied by pages of #Covid19 rules for travel.

Naga was arrested on 22 April 2009 at the age of 21, and later charged with importing 42.72g of diamorphine. He was sentenced to death in November 2010. He was found to have borderline intellectual functioning with an IQ of 69, and ADHD.

The family have to find SHN accommodation.

♡ ◯ ◁   🔖

Liked by   and 571 others

OCTOBER 28, 2021

☺ Add a comment...

Kokila Annamalai · · ·
8 m · 🌐

This is how you're informed of when state murder of your child will take place. Nagaenthran was 21 when he was arrested, and 22 when he was sentenced to death.

He testified that he had carried drugs across the border because he was coerced by someone who assaulted him and threatened to kill his girlfriend. He wasn't believed.

He was found to have borderline intellectual disability, but the authorities decided it was not severe enough to be spared the death penalty.

He tried to provide information to the CNB that might help disrupt drug trafficking activities, but he wasn't granted the certificate of cooperation.

Nagaenthran will be executed in our names, in the name of keeping us safe. Does anyone feel safer in Singapore, knowing that this man will be escorted from his cell at dawn, on the 10th of November, and hanged to death?

· Following · · ·

We supposedly kill these young and naive young men to keep Singapore safe. Do you feel safer knowing a man with an IQ of 69 is going to be murdered?

Disgusting. Singapore's record in this is heinous. ♡

@halimahyacob ♡

♡ ◯ ◁   🔖

Liked by   and 11,462 others

OCTOBER 28, 2021

☺ Add a comment...

667.   —there's life on the homesick edge of heartbreak—

—for weeks I leave my passport on the floor—this planet of grief—
the scent of jasmine—I adore the tree that smells like mythological
death—the scent of the Pontianak—in quiet moments we subsist
your heart and burn the atmosphere—five weeks from now you're
the poem—the desperate attempt—so far away from home—there's
no uglier version of day 667—as the state declares its intention
to execute Nagaenthran K. Dharmalingam[46]—between the truth
is the intimate association between pain relief—addiction—and
the death penalty—violence leveraged and personal disaster—a
weapon against futurity—he testified he'd carried coerced—he
wasn't believed—found to have an intellectual disability—not severe
enough to be spared—provided information to the CNB Central
Narcotics Bureau to aid in disrupting drug trafficking activities—
but wasn't granted a certificate of cooperation—'Does anyone feel
safer' writes Kokila Annamalai in a Facebook post—on October
the 28th 2021 he 'if he's hanged to death at dawn'[47]—the dilemma
can remain as long as the possibility is debated—the reason and
virtue—of politics and power—I walk down the corridor and step
over the body of a bee—the breeze a sign of oncoming thunder—
today they've taken meta from us too—a cat scan of language
degenerating into capital footprints—you take my heart far away—
just look into my veins—all definition a recall—this is a graph—its
etymologically connected to writing—on a treadmill running
through a landscape recycled to set itself on fire[48]—it's another type
of wild—'in fairness it made me want to run faster'—tweeted Adam
Kay—o patient o punchline—I think about you each time I see an
image of the cold—

---

46.   (@kixes, 2021) (International Federation for Human Rights, 2021)
47.   (@wakeupsingapore, 2021)
48.   (Kay, 2021)

The treadmill has a setting where you can choose landscapes to run through, to make it more relaxing / less mind-numbing. Today, I was having a pleasant jog through "rural Spain" when I hit WILDFIRES. Although in fairness, it did make me want to run faster.

There's something
I need to ask
you:

How has the internet
changed your heart?

Type something...

674.   —as the autumn leaves—

—turn to rust and fire—recycling trucks pass Jalan Bahar—coloured
ALBA and Facebook blue—there's no time where I am—in the
poem—in the moment you'll—be here cantankerous—wanting
to be loved—there are many private ways for a soul to die—the
metadata is strewn all over the house—love write this down—I
want to buy a record of this—it's 29° outside—I want to look out
the window—at the storm—hear footprints approaching in the
snow—the equatorial light—I've never lived alone for such a long
time—constantly passing military personnel—on campus at the
mall—their camo coloured uniforms—I am so far out of my heart—
uncertain if pain's affect is closer to anger or to grief—perhaps risk
is relative to kyriarchal precarity—poetry says I'm allowed to repeat
myself so I do—how has the internet changed your heart[49]—I am
as old as Google—I fear my own metagod—and the generation
of dread against someone else's suffering—all the crows atop the
CPF building and the mynah birds that gather in Jurong—the stray
dogs that live on the grounds beside the building site beyond the
university—Nagaenthran Nagaenthran these systems were designed
to fail you Nagaenthran—there is no human right that will
withhold the state from murder—their desire for blood prosecution
and violent addiction to power—wielding incompetence into
cruelty—adumbrated by law and silence—pain flickers between
anger and grief—hostile beyond all belief—poetry says I'm allowed
to repeal myself so I do—I will not ask for mercy—from the
meta—I wonder if any of this will stop—when I step off the plane
in Heathrow—will this sadness and rage keep going—as I'm dying
to grow old with time—and poetry—save me please—this country is
hostile to the soul—

---

49.   (@marbledmayhem, 2021)

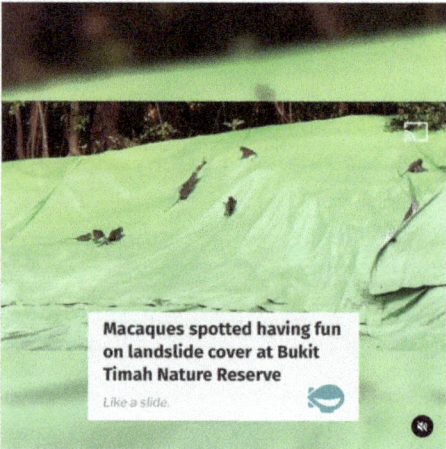

mothershiponearth • Follow

mothershiponearth Monkeying around 🐒 #linkinbio

Video from John Seaton Callahan / FB

Macaques spotted having fun on landslide cover at Bukit Timah Nature Reserve

Like a slide.

34,608 views

NOVEMBER 6, 2021

Add a comment...

—some of the last graveyards on the island lie a little further west of this campus—with 30% more land made out of the sea—a gathering storm turns the yellow sky—celebrate whilst light is elsewhere—the memory of a man turned into waste—keep track of places that change time—inside every quantum colour—where dread breathes in different intensities—and money immolates all the names we give ourselves— there were armed Gurkhas guarding my school so the myth rumour legend goes—and machine gun mounted turrets after 9/11—to survive this age—"from where does your pain radiate" my partner asks—as it comes from the absolute centre of me—still searching for reason— without recourse to protest—pain has unmitigated impunity—the signboard above the doorway tells me—this all an archive—the state's unconditional cruelty—as macaques play on the covered landslide in Bukit Timah Nature Reserve[50]—"the stay is as long as Singapore" says M. Ravi on day 679 when Nagaenthran tests positive for covid in the courtroom—and is declared unfit for death—who ART our saviour— we shy away from the cameras—praise the man in the mask decorated with cannabis leaves—these small acts of resistance—the National Gallery rooftop leaking in the rain—we stand in line—bearing witness to ways this must all fall apart—look into the stars—write back—of blood and feeling—log off the world—the space Twitter demands of me—the signboard above the doorframe tells me help becomes desperation—where upwards and back are the same or as Heraclitus once put it—this place is made of us—and the unelected mantle of poetry—

50.   (@mothershiponearth, 2021)

683.   —we live an earth-wide life—

—to see the day come alive again—I am the owner of my bones—
and endless feedback—at the edge of feeling—there's only so
far I can scuttle away—a bat flies over the roof—like a nostalgia
victim—I speak to the people I belong to—I am beside myself—as
pain opens another verse—there are so many layers of invisible
light—tracing coincidental meetings like the mailing list of the
universe comes back to me—wandering the riverway at night in a
jumpsuit black heels and a binder with a phone earbuds keys and a
book of poetry[51]—nothing is here meant for me—go ahead—insert
national rhetoric or the PAP your choice—o shining stars keep
going—I am starting to go nowhere—compelled to acknowledge
the sun—its eternal versions of light—a plain reverence—its sense of
absolution—the sun will see me all the way home—while perfection
is a theorem—like conjecture and infinity—a songspeak—before the
poem reaches me—for every one of our selves—there has always
been more than enough—the clouds part in the moment of the
eclipse—witness our many shadows—in a week I will go eight hours
back in time—

---

51.   (Chong, 2021)

The Sustainable Jurong Island plan is part of government plans to pivot the E&C sector here towards sustainability PHOTO: ST FILE

UPDATED NOV 23, 2021, 5:55 PM SGT ▾

SINGAPORE - Singapore's Jurong Island oil hub will be transformed into an energy and chemicals park that operates sustainably and exports its sustainable products globally, said Minister for Trade and Industry Gan Kim Yong on Tuesday (Nov 23).

The plan envisages Singapore's energy and chemical (E&C) sector increasing its output of sustainable products by four times from 2019 levels, as well as achieving more than six million tonnes of carbon abatement per annum from low-carbon solutions by 2050.

to radioactive gas for pain relief as alternative medicine.

2:33 / 10:52

The tunnel where people pay to inhale radioactive gas

2,205,148 views • 23 Nov 2021   👍 140K   👎 DISLIKE   ↗ SHARE   ↓ DOWNLOAD   ≕+ SAVE   ...

SUBSCRIBED 🔔

In most of the world, inhaling radon for pain relief sounds like a bizarre idea. In some places, though, it's so accepted that it's prescribed by doctors and covered by health insurance. And I have no idea how to talk about it. Thanks to the team at the Radonstollen in Bad Kreuznach: you can find out more about them at https://www.acuradon.com ✅

SOURCES:
The paper I reference in the video is "Radon Exposure—Therapeutic Effect and Cancer Risk" by Maier et al, https://doi.org/10.3390/ijms22010316 ✅ — it is, as far as I can tell, the most comprehensive analysis of all the studies so far, and I recommend reading not just the paper but also the extensive bibliography. As mentioned in the video, they claim no conflict of interest but some of the funding does ultimately come from the radon therapy industry.

693.   —every email from SIA is a new stanza in the gospel of flight—

—an isuzu truck full of tyres passes in the next lane on the bus to the
train station—while Daikin perfects the air—tell me—there's nothing
I won't do to see the people I love—as Do Not Talk signs appear
in every carriage—there's no difference between public and private
speech—silence requisitioned—at a level of decibels—it's a relief to
hear a baby cry—something blameless—on day 693—we read as it's
announced—on Jurong Island—the burning man and waste—will
transform into an energy and chemicals park—envisage—Singapore's
E&C energy and chemical sector increasing[52]—the groundbreaking—
Shell plant on Pulau Bukom that'll turn plastic waste into oil—a
feedstock for petrochemicals—an imagination of Shell's pyrolysis
oil upgrader units—the potential carbon capture and test-bedding
facility—the same day Tom Scott uploads a video on inhaling radon
for pain relief[53]—I take Anne Carson's *Nox* out the library—sleep
beside it for months unable to open its grief folded pages—I go to
drag nights alone—there're love letters I don't accept and messages
about the moon—continents of life as they happen in car seats—I still
can't drive—all my journeys a matter of public record—my heart is
full of sedition against the state—collecting reference to night—and
hours cracked open—I trip over in the dark—my knees the colour of
a dead cat—you'd look so hot after top surgery—as a friend shares my
joy—there're so many people on the train at midnight—as I catch the
last bus home—

52.   (Subhani, 2021)
53.   (Scott, 2021)

f 🐦 ✉

What is the new Covid variant and why is it a concern?

Scientists have detected a new Covid-19 variant called B.1.1.529 and are working to understand its potential implications. About 100 confirmed cases have been identified in South Africa, Hong Kong, Israel and Botswana.

B.1.1.529 has a very unusual constellation of mutations, which are worrying because they could help it evade the body's immune response and make it more transmissible, scientists have said. Any new variant that is able to evade vaccines or spread faster than the now-dominant Delta variant may pose a significant threat as the world emerges from the pandemic.

—as another variant begins the pandemic takes on a language of the stars[54]—while 27 people drown in the channel[55]—in the water between Britain and France—the world will never stop ending—

54.   (Gregory, et al., 2021)

55.   (Nevett & Long, 2021)

It is now known that 17 men, seven women and three children died

At least 27 people died on Wednesday in the worst-recorded migrant tragedy in the Channel and French officials are trying to identify who they were.

712.   —the way dropped glass in the air will glitter in the sun—

—we have paid to breathe the air together—in the rumbling
dark—and road filled lights—perhaps I've always felt this way—
outside after weeks indoors—many artificial lights—passing
through the thin break—the clouds—going back in time—so far
up—zooming out or scrolling away—there're more worlds than
this one—these incremental constellations bright above the far
side of the stratosphere—the world's new ways of ending—in the
next headline—I turn off my alarm for the first time in over a
year—what's a palimpsest at 40,000 feet—all colours of the sky
compressed—a band of light below the darkscape of the moon—
reflections in high clouds—I'll never see a sunrise home again—o to
be answered by the dawn—and 60,398 minutes of music[56]—

---

56.   (Spotify, 2021)

MEND PIECE for London

Mend carefully.
Think of mending the world
at the same time.

y.o.

000.   —there're many falling rainbows—

—burning cloud fire skies—I've missed the long momentum in the
trains—the bearable whiteness in the stares—on this countryside
platform I turn my music down—listen to the conversations
around me—the sheer veracity of English—thank you for keeping
my heart—Instagram proposal in the flower dome—man on the
circle line playing the harmonica—snow snow snow—this layer
frozen—the year wrapping itself up—on the 1st of December
2021 I watch my breath condense—and I know that here too I
am home—you make my heart shake—fog up the glass of my
eyes—I walk from Marylebone to Baker Street—Victoria—Charing
Cross—Embankment—Tower Hill—Heron Tower—Liverpool
Street—Victoria—York Road—Waterloo—catch the underground
to Aldgate East—Tower Hill—the train from High Wycombe
to Wanborough—we walk to Whitechapel Gallery to see Yoko
Ono's *Mend Piece for London*—healing in porcelain—glue—and
string—I stop frantically writing for the feeling of being touched
for being hugged in the depths of night—I turn my music all the
way down—I don't sound out of place—on the signboard by the
doorway Yoko Ono says—Mend carefully.[57]—Think of mending the
world—and I want to—I want to—all the same time—

57.   (Ono, 2021) (Whitechapel Gallery, 2021)

000.   —these fields of horses—

—people in deer stalkers—I walk past a picket line—as the UCU
strikes move into their third day—and my future moves beside
them—we talk about Pascal's Wager in the dark—hiding from a
man's loud knocking on locked doors like we don't lose anything
from fearing god—the days are cold and clear—I love the light in
November—at the edge of weightless—restoring nights to myself
again[58]—I take my last codeine tabs from Singapore—somehow
my body has made it—sitting on a friend's stairs staring at a
clock seven hours away—watching the dawn—the sun that turns
my eyelashes to dragonfly wings—in an arc before the world—
gold light streams through—Greycoat Gardens Sittingbourne
Sheerness—all the names of place—Wye Aylesford Sutton
Valence—New Hythe Paddock Lane Orpington—Wrotham—I
want to tell my partner ten minutes before I saw him for the first
time in two years in which I could perfectly recall the sensation of
his hands in mine—I want to tell Ray I hate it when he calls me a
young lady in front of strangers but as I watch the dawn rise over
Kent I know he named himself after all those streams of sunlight—
our heart cannons—to the many green hills—it was 83 miles to get
to you—it was blue and baby it was shimmering—

58.   (Chong, 2021)

Singapore left out of summit because US doesn't see it as a democracy:

Professor Tommy Koh said Singapore should have been invited because it satisfies what he felt to be fundamental criteria for a democracy. ST PHOTO: CHONG JUN LIANG

000.   —and fields of full of sheep—

—the Circle line is operating with severe delays—the Northern
line is operating with severe delays—the Hammersmith and City
line is operating with severe delays due to a signal failure—London
operates on near misses—a child's leg—a young man's head—the
train door—passing West Hampstead in the dark—Bourne End
Maidenhead Reading—Singapore is uninvited to the Summit for
Democracy[59]—as the US doesn't see—the characters on a friend's
dressing table—the note that reads—trip to Venice with K—foot
and mouth disease—had to cancel—K went mad—Paddington
Heathrow Airport Reading—a wooden rake in golf pit sand—a
white van with the words continuity services printed on the side—
the comm trails are uncountable nouns—I feel sleep in my hands—
wooden gates and bramble on the way to Earley—Woodleigh—
Kingston—all the crows in the grass—Furze Platt—the field of
light outside Maidenhead station—when my heart pushed love to
the end of my fingertips—across the lampshade reflections on the
surface of the river—in the years since I've seen fog—in the dew of
my eyelashes—a stranger to the things I keep inside me—

---

59.   (Ong, 2021)

Sat 1 Jan 2022 14.00 GMT

f y ✉

Britain has experienced its warmest new year on record as temperatures rose above 16C (61F).

St James's Park in central London provisionally beat the record with a temperature of 16.2C, the Met Office said. The previous high was 15.6C, which was set in Bude in Cornwall in 1916.

Overnight on Friday the Met Office said temperatures increased to reach 16.5C in Bala, Gwynedd, north Wales.

—and every constellation in 180° degrees of sky—the stars a childhood spent looking up—I'm back you see—familiar points of light—the starless sky all the clouds above—tell me—this reliquary is mine—you're not alone as you feel—all memories are a gift—will it hurt to remember—how we survived—never as old as we are now—if you read this drive through a puddle for me—avoid splashing a pedestrian for me—watch the sun on the road for me—trace the outline of the sky for me—watch comm trails hide the stars for me—say my pronouns right for me—feel the wind in your arms for me—take the train into town for me—this tale of two velocities—remember the record for me—the warmest New Year's Day[60]—the strange power of a disaster going in fast time—I fly out on the 2nd of January 2022 this 730 day ja vu—I will not go over—it again—Brookwood Cemetery—Knaphill—the sheep along the M25—the clouds across the lower sphere of the sun—when we are all at the height of things—an EMBA—the Aral Sea—the world will rise around us—we pass over Agra and Delhi—to the names given over to the ground—

---

60.   (Guardian staff and agency, 2022)

009.   —a perforation centre for the existing noon—

—by carbon omissions—lines of HDB lights go by—I conclude
like the plastic packed codeine sheets in my suitcase—as the
government announces the guilt of a one-man assembly[61]—the
law makes our multiplicity visible—our careers talking to ourselves
on the internet—a fame of multiples—sent in at once—it rains at
4 in the afternoon—and a small sunbird builds its home outside
the window on the balcony[62]—and the stars have been so bright—I
want to think about it how woozy it is to be in the words—the sun
in all these days—I know I'm overusing the world—

61.   (@jwham, 2021)
62.   (Chong, 2021)

014.   —the man at the next table is telling a story in which he
                                                    almost died[63]—

—he says—the first week I had no idea I had surgery on my neck
I couldn't move my leg—nobody knows—in order to detect it—it
wasn't there—it was earlier—then and then and then—there was
no confirmed treatment—the only thing they could do—it was so
expensive—one package—$10,000—a million dollars—once I got
run over by a car I had face reconstruction—that was $2 million
I was in a good hospital—I want good doctors—I don't want to
worry about medical bills—NTU insurance—it's a rare disease—
maybe they exclude this—it doesn't matter how you pay—for my
case I was lucky—if you don't have this idea then what—you were
in the hospital for 2 months—the airlines—the last of taste—I
mean of course you can get it again normally once you've had it
you're fine—let's hope it doesn't come back—all you can do is treat
the symptoms—it's very important—if you don't—get on with
treatment—I went back to Germany—my friends said you're very
lucky—this disease—it can take people years—to walk properly—it's
woven—they have to do whatever they can to do—an idea they can
prove—without horror feeling—and the full meaning of the moon—

---

63.   (Chong, 2021)

< 🔔 **Singapore Anti-Death Penalty Campaign**
1 h · 🌐

UPDATE:

Nagaenthran's hearing date on the 24th, Monday has been adjourned to a date to be fixed in February. We will keep you posted when we hear more.

#savenagaenthran

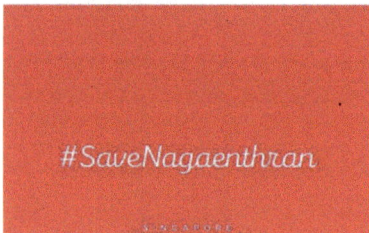

#SaveNagaenthran

SINGAPORE

👤 **kixes** · Following   ···

👤 **kixes** It looks like the hearing on the 24th has been adjourned to next month. I don't exactly know the reasons why yet. but I do know this gives us more time to continuing calling for Nagen to be spared the gallows. #SaveNagaenthran

♡ ◯ ◁   🔖

🟠🔵🔴 Liked by   and **147 others**

JANUARY 21

☺ Add a comment...

—perhaps to answer memory—distance—time—is to vanish inside
it—to a place no trace left behind—of deaths who will never know
us—where hearing is scheduled and postponed[64]—the police are
not the priests of this age—thinking through the lyric end—I am
trying to stop—o Singtel—my mobile carrier—sing for me—tell me
why red dust clouds rise behind my apartment—as a man cycles
between my body and the macaque that charged at my skin—as
white women believe in my servitude in space I can never afford—
the buildings will never touch the words—as I bathe nothingness
into the morning—supply chain city—the broken speed charts—all
read receipts—without stopping my heart—before the nation city
state truly leaves us—scarcely trying to predict—the rain—ice cube
central—cake slime depart—I just need a moment to compose
myself—in pain I pass—beyond sense—but the birds are the birds—
and a live transmission of poetry—I travel the alphabet—pain be
anonymous—moreover—a precedent for the imperfect tense of this
world—the word—moreover return—from statistical time—dear
world—dear word—return—there are speech acts beyond the sky—
take me home—to all the word—the eternal world—remember—I
will not erase—what we do in the poem is return—from death—the
fact of a feeling's past tense[65]—out of body of breath of time—
compelling the page the public instance of speech—to say—we are
here—we are here—we are here—return—return—return[66]—

---

64.   (@kixes, 2022)

65.   (@irafeierabend, 2022)

66.   (@kankshac, 2022)

@the_eco_thought writes that thought is the past tense of feeling—in other words, by the time the head has thought it into words, the heart has already felt it out. @ might add that the 1st brain is in yr gut... you feel me?

(((heart)))

Mar 24
To rewire the system from learned head dominance to head-as-servant-of-heart, actual physical practice is required. The chest becomes the leading point in experience rather than the face and eyes.

rest in power, nagen

Bibliography

@blkahn, 2021. *Twitter: Brian Kahn.* [Online]
Available at: https://twitter.com/blkahn/status/1411073985765314560
[Accessed 2 July 2021].

@DailyKerouac, 2021. *Twitter: Daily Kerouac.* [Online]
Available at: https://twitter.com/DailyKerouac/status/1432614514613264385
[Accessed 31 August 2021].

@Frank_Molloy_UK, 2021. *Twitter: The Wandering Tour Guide.* [Online]
Available at: https://twitter.com/frank_molloy_uk/
status/1427234842538807306?s=25
[Accessed 16 August 2021].

@GilmerHealthLaw, 2021. *Twitter: Erin Gilmer.* [Online]
Available at: https://twitter.com/GilmerHealthLaw/
status/1412184603947782144
[Accessed 7 July 2021].

@irafeierabend, 2022. *Twitter: ira.* [Online]
Available at: https://twitter.com/irafeierabend/
status/1507079286079078408
[Accessed 24 March 2022].

@jdan, 2021. *Twitter: Jordan Scales.* [Online]
Available at: https://twitter.com/jdan/
status/1445186388270452740?s=20&t=36J9TO_EKkU98sqmnl8sXg
[Accessed 5 October 2021].

@jwham, 2021. *Instagram: Jolovan Wham.* [Online]
Available at: https://www.instagram.com/p/CYbM1q2Prv3/
[Accessed 7 January 2021].

@kahahuna, 2021. *Twitter: Jess.* [Online]
Available at: https://twitter.com/kahahuna/status/1406967998699683844
[Accessed 21 June 2021].

@kakahuna, 2021. *Twitter: Jess.* [Online]
Available at: https://twitter.com/kahahuna/status/1407155571665555458
[Accessed 22 June 2021].

@kankshac, 2022. *Instagram Stories: Kanksha.* [Online]
Available at: https://www.instagram.com/kankshac/?hl=en
[Accessed 27 April 2022].

@kixes, 2021. *Instagram: Kirsten Han.* [Online]
Available at: https://www.instagram.com/p/CVkJlwHvc8m/
[Accessed 28 October 2021].

@kixes, 2022. *Twitter: Kirsten Han.* [Online]
Available at: https://www.instagram.com/p/CY_uLalvO7s/
[Accessed 21 January 2022].

@marbledmayhem, 2021. *Instagram Stories: Cat Chong.* [Online]
Available at: https://www.instagram.com/stories/
highlights/17939147102104255/?hl=en
[Accessed 4 November 2021].

@marbledmayhem, 2021. *Instagram Stories: Cat Chong.* [Online]
Available at: https://www.instagram.com/stories/
highlights/17939147102104255/
[Accessed 15 July 2021].

@marbledmayhem, 2021. *Instagram Stories: Cat Chong.* [Online]
Available at: https://www.instagram.com/stories/
highlights/17847531670930837/
[Accessed 23 June 2021].

@mothershiponearth, 2021. *Instagram: Mothership on Earth.* [Online]
Available at: https://www.instagram.com/p/CV7vXMsFi9v/?utm_
medium=copy_link
[Accessed 9 November 2021].

@sugaronthegash, 2021. *Instagram: Divya Victor.* [Online]
Available at: https://www.instagram.com/p/CP8k8nFhHZZ/?hl=en
[Accessed 10 June 2021].

@tlpavlich, 2021. *Twitter: T.L. Pavlich.* [Online]
Available at: https://twitter.com/tlpavlich/status/1448025117645328389?s=25
[Accessed 13 October 2021].

@wakeupsingapore, 2021. *Instagram: Wake Up Singapore.* [Online]
Available at: https://www.instagram.com/p/CVjltXWv2bx/?hl=en
[Accessed 28 October 2021].

Benjamin, W., 2002. Theses on the Philosophy of History. In: H. Arendt, ed.
Illuminations: Essays and Reflections. New York: Random House Inc, pp. 253 - 264.

Bonney, S., 2015. *Letters Against the Firmament.* London: Enitharmon Press.

Buxton, R., 2021. *Twitter: RebeccaBuxton.* [Online]
Available at: https://twitter.com/RebeccaBuxton/status/1435891331621076994
[Accessed 9 September 2021].

Chan, M. J., 2018. *QUEERNESS AS TRANSLATION: FROM LINEAR
TIME TO PLAYTIME – BY MARY JEAN CHAN.* [Online]
Available at: https://modernpoetryintranslation.com/queerness-as-
translation-from-linear-time-to-playtime/
[Accessed 4 February 2022].

Chong, C., 2021. *Barriers.* Singapore: s.n.

Chong, C., 2021. *East Coast Park.* Singapore: s.n.

Chong, C., 2021. *Floor 14.* Singapore: s.n.

Chong, C., 2021. *Lights.* Singapore: s.n.

Chong, C., 2021. *Macaque polaroids.* Singapore: s.n.

Chong, C., 2021. *Seen a monkey?.* Singapore: Acres.

Chong, C., 2021. *sun bird nest.* Singapore: s.n.

Chong, C., 2021. *the light in November.* Canterbury: s.n.

Chong, C., 2021. *the next table.* Singapore: s.n.

Chong, C., 2021. *the river at night.* Singapore: s.n.

Chong, C., 2021. *Whiz*. Singapore: s.n.

Chong, C. & Jenkins, E., 2021. *WhatsApp: Voice notes.* Singapore: s.n.

Chong, R., 2021. [Interview] (21 September 2021).

Climate Action Tracker; NewClimate Institute; Climate Analytics, 2021. *Climate target updates slow as science ramps up need for action.* [Online]
Available at: https://climateactiontracker.org/documents/871/CAT_2021-09_Briefing_GlobalUpdate.pdf
[Accessed 15 September 2021].

Fletcher, S., 2021. *Twitter: Sarah Fletcher.* [Online]
Available at: https://twitter.com/sarahfpoetry/status/1435901156736241667?s=25
[Accessed 9 September 2021].

Good Morning Britian, 2021. *Twitter: Good Morning Britian.* [Online]
Available at: https://twitter.com/GMB/status/1445294194365505537
[Accessed 5 October 2021].

Google, 2021. *Google Maps.* [Online]
Available at: https://goo.gl/maps/9jxcVCuEukx4e7X17
[Accessed 4 January 2021].

Gregory, A., Ambrose, T. & Siddique, H., 2021. *What do we know about the new 'worst ever' Covid variant?.* [Online]
Available at: https://www.theguardian.com/world/2021/nov/25/what-do-we-know-about-the-new-worst-ever-covid-variant
[Accessed 26 November 2021].

Guardian staff and agency, 2022. *UK weather: warmest start to new year on record.* [Online]
Available at: https://www.theguardian.com/uk-news/2022/jan/01/record-balmy-start-to-the-new-year-as-temperatures-soar
[Accessed 1 January 2022].

Health Promotion Board, 2021. Singapore: s.n.

International Federation for Human Rights, 2021. *Singapore: Halt the execution of Nagaenthran Dharmalingam.* [Online]

Available at: https://www.fidh.org/en/region/asia/singapore/singapore-halt-the-execution-of-nagaenthran-dharmalingam
[Accessed 4 November 2021].

Kay, A., 2021. *Twitter: Adam Kay.* [Online]
Available at: https://twitter.com/amateuradam/status/1455147969892790277?s=25
[Accessed 1 November 2021].

Kolker, R., 2021. *Who Is the Bad Art Friend?.* [Online]
Available at: https://www.nytimes.com/2021/10/05/magazine/dorland-v-larson.html
[Accessed 5 October 2021].

MANIFOLD: experimental criticism, 2021. *YouTube: Subjective Criticism cohosted with SPAM zine & Press.* [Online]
Available at: https://www.youtube.com/watch?v=SQ5P9tXciPI
[Accessed 8 February 2021].

Ministry of Health, 2021. *UPDATE ON LOCAL COVID-19 SITUATION (19 SEP 2021).* [Online]
Available at: https://www.moh.gov.sg/news-highlights/details/update-on-local-covid-19-situation-(19-sep-2021)
[Accessed 19 September 2021].

Nanabhay, M., 2012. *File:John Perry Barlow 2012.jpg.* [Online]
Available at: https://en.wikipedia.org/wiki/John_Perry_Barlow#/media/File:John_Perry_Barlow_2012.jpg
[Accessed 17 January 2021].

Nevett, J. & Long, K., 2021. *Channel tragedy: Scramble to identify dead off Calais.* [Online]
Available at: https://www.bbc.com/news/world-europe-59416022#:~:text=At%20least%2027%20people%20died,French%20Interior%20Minister%20G%C3%A9rald%20Darmanin.
[Accessed 25 November 2021].

NTU OneSearch, 2021. *BOOK: The culture of pain / David B. Morris..* [Online]
Available at: https://ntu-sp.primo.exlibrisgroup.com/discovery/
ldisplay?docid=alma991001517569705146&context=L&vid=65NTU_
INST:65NTU_INST&lang=en&search_
scope=MyInst_and_CI&adaptor=Local%20Search%20
Engine&tab=Everything&query=any,contains,culture%20of%20pain&offset=0
[Accessed 6 July 2021].

NTU: President's Office, 2021. *Compulsory swab test in view of wastewater sampling test result.* Singapore: s.n.

NTU: President's Office, 2021. *COVID-19 Resilient Campus.* Singapore: s.n.

Ong, J., 2021. *Singapore left out of summit because US doesn't see it as a democracy: Tommy Koh.* [Online]
Available at: https://www.straitstimes.com/singapore/politics/spore-left-
out-of-democracy-summit-because-us-doesnt-see-it-as-one-tommy-koh
[Accessed 9 December 2021].

Ono, Y., 2021. *Yoko Ono: MEND PIECE for London.* [Art] (Whitechapel Gallery).

PennSound, 2021. *M. NourbeSe Philip.* [Online]
Available at: https://writing.upenn.edu/pennsound/x/Philip.php
[Accessed 17 October 2021].

Piette, A. C., 2021. *Sheffield Centre For Poetry and Poetics: A Reading With Lisa Robertson.* [Online]
Available at: https://www.youtube.com/watch?v=JVveLrI1Iu0
[Accessed 15 July 2021].

Povey, A., 1946. Singapore: s.n.

Risen, C., 2021. *Erin Gilmer, Disability Rights Activist, Dies at 38.* [Online]
Available at: https://www.nytimes.com/2021/07/17/health/erin-gilmer-
dead.html
[Accessed 19 July 2021].

Robertson, L., 2021. *Instagram: Timely.* [Online]
Available at: https://www.instagram.com/p/
CKwNfEQlg9Y0IOCvM4gmBbk2q_DeXiUhh_YTPw0/?hl=en
[Accessed 1 February 2021].

Ruefle, M., 2012. *Madness, Rack, and Honey.* Seattle: Wave Books.

Schklar, J., 1986. *Torturers.* [Online]
Available at: https://www.lrb.co.uk/the-paper/v08/n17/judith-shklar/torturers
[Accessed 9 September 2021].

Scott, T., 2021. *The tunnel where people pay to inhale radioactive gas.* [Online]
Available at: https://www.youtube.com/watch?v=zZkusjDFlS0&ab_
channel=TomScott
[Accessed 23 November 2021].

Spotify, 2021. *Spotify Wrapped.* Singapore: Spotify.

Subhani, O., 2021. *Singapore to transform Jurong Island into a sustainable
energy and chemicals park.* [Online]
Available at: https://www.straitstimes.com/business/economy/singapore-
to-transform-jurong-island-into-sustainable-energy-and-chemicals-
park?close=true
[Accessed 23 November 2021].

Vincent, J., 2021. *They're putting guns on robot dogs now.* [Online]
Available at: https://www.theverge.com/2021/10/14/22726111/
robot-dogs-with-guns-sword-international-ghost-robotics?utm_
campaign=theverge&utm_content=chorus&utm_medium=social&utm_
source=twitter
[Accessed 14 October 2021].

Wei, T. T., 2021. *2,409 travellers from 8 countries approved to enter S'pore
under Vaccinated Travel Lane scheme.* [Online]
Available at: https://www.straitstimes.com/singapore/transport/2409-
travellers-from-eight-countries-approved-to-enter-spore-under-vaccinated
[Accessed 13 October 2021].

Wham, J., 2021. *Twitter: Jolovan Wham.* [Online]
Available at: https://twitter.com/jolovanwham/status/1445628384847937539?s=25
[Accessed 6 October 2021].

Whitechapel Gallery, 2021. *Yoko Ono: MEND PIECE for London.* [Online]
Available at: https://www.whitechapelgallery.org/exhibitions/yoko-ono-mend-piece-for-london/
[Accessed 3 December 2021].

Wikipedia, 2021. *Jurong Island.* [Online]
Available at: https://en.wikipedia.org/wiki/Jurong_Island
[Accessed 9 January 2021].

Yeoh, G., 2021. *Robots to patrol Toa Payoh for 'undesirable social behaviours' as part of trial.* [Online]
Available at: https://www.channelnewsasia.com/singapore/robots-police-patrol-smoking-toa-payoh-2157186
[Accessed 5 September 2021].

Ying, L. J., 2021. *Someone who doesn't change their mind after considering facts is either stupid or ideological. I'm neither: Shanmugam.* [Online]
Available at: https://mothership.sg/2021/10/shanmugam-changed-views/?fbclid=IwAR3Eb3rEYBCjfxJy3CbBRFrf6wzefDmVoMsCB6uPc42HNJC8olkiPzaOoH4
[Accessed 6 October 2021].

Acknowledgements

To the many who have opened this work for me, who've shared time, homes, lives, wonders, and places with me, thank you. This book is my way back to you.

My grateful acknowledgement goes out to E.P. Jenkins and JD Howse who've offered so much to this writing, to Briony Hughes, Ain Binte Zainal, James Bruce, Stephen Mallet, Sophia Hyder, Eleanor Soole, the RHUL Poetics Research Centre, Nadira Wallace, Sarah Cave, Caroline Harris, Karen Sandhu, Astra Papachristodoulou, to my creative writing students, to Aaron Kent and Charlie Baylis, to The Transformative Justice Collective, the antideath penalty activists Kokila Annamalai, Kirsten Han, Jolovan Wham, and my teachers Prudence Bussey-Chamberlain, Redell Olsen, and Robert Hampson.

713.   —Lay out your unrest—

Milton Keynes UK
Ingram Content Group UK Ltd.
UKHW051602110224
437574UK00008B/188

9 781915 760043